What Was
the Hindenburg?

by Janet B. Pascal

illustrated by David Groff

Grosset & Dunlap
An Imprint of Penguin Group (USA) LLC

For Jim Lewis, because it's his favorite disaster—JBP

GROSSET & DUNLAP
Published by the Penguin Group
Penguin Group (USA) LLC, 375 Hudson Street, New York, New York 10014, USA

USA | Canada | UK | Ireland | Australia | New Zealand | India | South Africa | China

penguin.com
A Penguin Random House Company

Library of Congress Cataloging-in-Publication Data is available.

ISBN 978-0-448-48119-7   10 9 8 7 6 5 4 3 2 1

Contents

What Was the *Hindenburg*?

On Thursday, May 6, 1937, a crowd gathered in Lakehurst, New Jersey. They were there to watch the airship *Hindenburg* land. Although the ship had arrived in Lakehurst several times before, it was still a thrilling sight. The *Hindenburg* was the first flying ship ever to carry passengers over the Atlantic Ocean to America.

A little while before
7:00 p.m., the *Hindenburg*
appeared. It was a kind of ship
called a *zeppelin*. This is a large balloon
on a hard frame, filled with a gas that is
lighter than air. It floats through the sky like
a helium balloon. To hold enough gas to stay
up, zeppelins had to be huge. The *Hindenburg*
was almost a sixth of a mile long. It was shaped

like a tube with rounded ends. Its surface was a shining silver. Despite its size, it floated lightly and quietly through the air, as much at home as a fish in water. As it began to sink gently toward the airfield, it was a beautiful sight.

More than a hundred workers were waiting on the field to help pull in the ship. The crew dropped two ropes to them. It seemed that the *Hindenburg* had finished another successful voyage.

What happened next would horrify the world and change the future of flying. Most people believed that these majestic, floating bubbles would soon carry passengers all over the world. Until May 6, 1937, it seemed they would someday rule the sky. But after that day, no passenger zeppelin ever flew again.

CHAPTER 1
Dreaming of Flight

For most of history, human flight was an impossible dream. It did not become real until 1783. The Montgolfier brothers in France designed a balloon filled with hot air. The balloon was made of fireproof fabric. It was about thirty-three feet across. Hot air weighs less than cold air.

Joseph-Michel Montgolfier

Jacques-Étienne Montgolfier

So the balloon floated. (People soon discovered that gas worked the same way.) If a basket was attached, it could lift things into the sky. The brothers didn't know if they could send people up in the basket. Maybe people wouldn't be able to live way up in the air. No human had ever been there. They sent up a sheep, a duck, and a rooster,

to make sure it was safe. The animals lived. On November 21, two men climbed into the balloon's basket. This was as many people as the balloon could easily lift. They floated for about five miles. These men were the first people ever to see earth from the sky.

Why Does a Gas Balloon Fly?

A gas-filled balloon rises because gas weighs less than air. The weight of the gas plus the balloon is less than the weight of the air in the space it occupies. If too much weight is added or too much gas is removed, it will not be able to rise. This is why helium party balloons float for a while and then slowly sink to the ground. The helium is escaping. When there is too little helium, the weight of the balloon pulls it to the ground. Gas-balloon pilots control their balloons by changing the weight. To raise the balloon, they throw something heavy overboard. To lower it, they let out some gas.

Soon all of Europe had "balloon fever." Everyone wanted to fly. But it was risky. A fire had to be kept burning in the basket so the air in the balloon would stay hot. And balloons were hard to steer. You might end up anywhere.

Only a few months after the first hot-air balloon flight, three Frenchmen launched a balloon filled with hydrogen. This is a gas six times lighter than hot air, so a balloon filled with it could float without needing a fire.

Gradually, people figured out how to steer balloons. In 1785, one flew over the English Channel.

Armies tried using balloons to observe the enemy, to get supplies over enemy lines, and to make maps. But for the next hundred years, they were mainly just an exciting way to have fun.

In 1863, a German count named Ferdinand von Zeppelin came to the United States. He was an army officer who was there to observe the American Civil War. After studying the battle-fields, he headed west. In Saint Paul, Minnesota, he met a pilot who had flown balloons for the Union army. Now this pilot took people up in his balloon. Zeppelin seized the chance. He never forgot the excitement of seeing the earth from the air for the first time. For the

Count Ferdinand von Zeppelin

next twenty years, it stayed in the back of his mind. He was sure the simple balloon he had flown in could be turned into something that would change the world.

CHAPTER 2
Lighter than Air

While Count Zeppelin was in the German army, he thought up a way to turn air balloons into real military tools. But he was too busy to follow up. Then in 1890, he got caught in a political struggle and had to resign. Now he had lots of free time. He began working out how someone could build an airship that would fly for long distances and go wherever the pilot wanted it to.

There are two ways to fly. One is heavier-than-air flying. This means flying like a bird. A bird weighs more than the air around it, but its wings keep it up. All modern airplanes are heavier-than-air fliers. With passengers and cargo, a Boeing 747 may weigh hundreds of tons. It flies using a principle of physics called *lift*. This means that if it is moving fast enough, the air under its wings will support it. A heavier-than-air ship cannot stand still in the sky. It must move forward or it will fall. By the end of the nineteenth century, no one had been able to make heavier-than-air flight work. Many people thought it wasn't possible.

Zeppelin was interested in lighter-than-air flying. This means the ship is filled with something that weighs less than air. It floats through the air, the same way a fish floats through water. It can float even if it is standing still. But it will not move unless it is pushed by some force. This can be a natural force like wind. Or it can be created by a propeller.

Count Zeppelin knew lighter-than-air flying was possible. He had been up in a balloon himself. In the years since then, inventors had figured out how to make better gas balloons. But there were still a few basic problems to be solved. Until these were fixed, balloons were exciting, but not very useful.

The main problem was how to balance size, weight, and power. The heavier an airship, the more gas was needed to lift it. So airships had to be as light as possible. But to push it forward, the ship needed some kind of engine. Engines were heavy. They used fuel, which was also heavy. The farther a ship had to travel, the more fuel it would need. Any airship that could be used for long trips or carrying cargo would need to lift a lot of weight. It would need a lot of gas to keep it lighter than air.

The more gas that was needed, the larger the balloon would have to be in order to hold it. But a balloon could be made only so big. The round shape of hot-air balloons made them hard to control. A football shape worked much better. This shape made steering easier and cut down on air resistance. But if it was built too big, it would stretch out of shape or bend in the middle.

Other Pioneers

In 1852, a Frenchman flew a balloon ship for seventeen miles using a steam engine. This was the first powered steerable airship. But the engine was heavy and couldn't put out much power. The ship moved very slowly. In 1888, a German clergyman was the first to use Gottlieb Daimler's powerful lightweight engine to run an airship. His first flights were successful, but in 1897 he was killed when sparks from the engine set fire to the hydrogen in the balloon. That same year, another German built the first rigid airship covered with aluminum. On its first flight, it crashed and was destroyed. Experimenting with airships was dangerous.

A second problem was danger from the gas. Balloons used hydrogen, the lightest of all gases. It was cheap and easy to make. However, hydrogen burns very easily. Even a small spark could make a balloon burst into flames. The engines that moved the ship forward ran on steam or fire. Both of these made sparks. So flying a hydrogen-filled balloon was very dangerous.

The automobile made the zeppelin possible. In 1886, Gottlieb Daimler created a new gasoline-burning engine. It put out a lot of power but didn't weigh much. It didn't make a lot of sparks. Daimler wanted a safe, light engine so he could build better cars. But Count Zeppelin saw that the engine was also perfect

Gottlieb Daimler

for lighter-than-air ships. He wanted the German government to build airships using Daimler's engine. He pushed his ideas so hard that people began to say he was crazy. They shouted insults at him as he walked down the street.

Finally, he realized that the government was not going to listen to him. If the ship was going to be built, he would have to build it himself.

CHAPTER 3
The Earliest Zeppelins

Count Zeppelin decided to start his own company. On a lake near the castle where he had grown up, he built a floating shed. Here, he could construct his huge flying ship. It took two years to build. He named it *Airship Zeppelin One* after himself. It was usually called LZ-1. The L stands for *Luftschiff*, the German word for airship.

Blimps, Zeppelins, and Other Airships

A *dirigible* is any kind of airship that can be steered. There are three main kinds. One built over a framework is called a rigid airship. Only rigid airships built by the Zeppelin Company can truly be called *zeppelins*. But the word is often used for any ship made like a zeppelin.

An airship built partly on a frame is called a *semirigid*. One with no framework is called a *blimp*. The word *blimp* probably comes from the sound a balloon makes when you tap it—*blimp*! Blimps can still be seen in the sky today. Most are used for advertising. The most famous modern one is the Goodyear Blimp, built by the Zeppelin Company's American partner.

On July 2, 1900, a large crew gathered on a barge in the middle of the lake. They held ropes attached to LZ-1. Slowly, they let the ropes out, and the ship rose gently into the air. It flew more than three miles in eighteen minutes, then landed safely. There were some problems. But the ship worked.

This very first zeppelin already had the same basic design that all later zeppelins right up through the *Hindenburg* would use. The balloon was built over a hard frame. This way, it could be made as big as needed, and the frame would keep it the right shape. The LZ-1 was 420 feet long and thirty-eight feet across. Its frame was made of aluminum. This metal is strong but very lightweight, so the frame did not add much to the weight of the ship. The gas was held in seventeen separate cells, making the ship safer. If one cell was damaged, the rest of the gas would still be safe. A cabin hung below the balloon to hold the captain and crew. Passengers stayed in the cabin.

The crew, however, moved all around the ship. They needed to check on the engine and the gas cells. Two motors also hung from the balloon. They operated the propellers that moved it forward.

LZ-1 flew two more times, but the government wasn't impressed. It didn't want to pay for the airship project. Count Zeppelin ran out of money and had to destroy his ship. But he did not give up. Finally, the government gave him enough money to try again. Five years later, he finished LZ-2. He hoped this ship had solved the first ship's problems. But he didn't get a chance to find out. On its very first flight, a motor failed, and LZ-2 had to make an emergency landing right after it took off. While it was on the ground, a storm tore it to pieces.

Count Zeppelin went ahead and built LZ-3.
This time, he added fins to the back of the ship
to hold it steady and steer it. LZ-3 could carry
eleven people. It made several successful flights.
One lasted eight hours. Finally, the German
government was interested. It asked Zeppelin to
prove his ship could survive a twenty-four-hour
flight. Then the government would buy it. For
the test flight, Zeppelin built an even better ship,
LZ-4. In a trial in July 1908, LZ-4 easily flew 240

miles, from Germany to Switzerland and back in twelve hours. Zeppelin was sure his ship would pass the army's test.

The twenty-four-hour trip started well. But soon the motor had problems. The ship had to touch down to be fixed. While it was tied up on the ground, a sudden summer storm tore it loose and threw it into a tree. It exploded in flames and was completely destroyed. Heartbroken, Zeppelin was ready to give up.

But something wonderful happened. The people of Germany had watched his airships flying overhead. They had fallen in love with them. People sent Zeppelin money from all over Germany. Rich or poor, everyone wanted him to build more flying ships. One child sent him the money he was supposed to put in the church collection plate—about ten cents.

Even though LZ-4 had failed the test, the army bought two zeppelins. But they still weren't sure how useful airships were. So Zeppelin decided to offer his ships to the citizens of Germany, instead. They had proved they believed in him.

CHAPTER 4
The World's First Airline

In 1909, Count Zeppelin created the world's first airline. It was called DELAG. One of his business partners was Hugo Eckener. After Zeppelin, Eckener is the most important person in the history of lighter-than-air flight. He had been in the crowd watching the first zeppelin fly. He was still part of the company when the last zeppelin made its final flight. At first, he wasn't interested in flying. He went to the zeppelin launch only because he was working as a newspaper reporter. But he fell in love with the huge silver balloons. He learned to fly one himself. When Count Zeppelin asked him to become flight director of the new company, he threw himself into a new life.

Hugo Eckener

Early Airplanes

Successful heavier-than-air flight came later than lighter-than-air flight. The very first airplanes were gliders. They didn't have any power source, but soared on air currents like a paper airplane. The first powered heavier-than-air flight was made by Wilbur and Orville Wright on December 17, 1903. The flight, in Kitty Hawk, North Carolina, lasted twelve seconds and went a little over 120 feet.

In 1908, the Wright brothers built an airplane that could stay up for an hour and a half. By the time World War I began in 1914, airplanes could fly well enough to be useful. They were used for fighting in the air and dropping bombs nearby. However, they could only stay up for a few hours before needing to refuel.

Wilbur Wright

Orville Wright

Zeppelin planned to build a fleet of airships to carry passengers all over Germany. His ships could fly twice as fast as the fastest trains. A trip from the southern part of Germany to Berlin might take eighteen hours or more on a train. Zeppelins could do it in four to nine hours. As more people began to ride them, Zeppelin hoped they would start to think of flying as a natural way to travel.

Only nine days after its first trip, DELAG's first zeppelin took some tourists on a sightseeing trip. In a sudden storm, the ship shot high up into the air. Then it sank into a forest, where it got stuck in the treetops. The crew had to let down a ladder so the passengers could climb to the ground. Fortunately, no one was hurt. Except for this one accident, everything went well. Soon the company had airships traveling between eight big cities.

The ships became more comfortable. The passenger cabins were made bigger. They began to look like fancy first-class railway carriages. They even had a washroom.

During the flight, passengers were served a meal, complete with caviar and champagne. The airline hired the world's first flight attendant to look after them.

The airships also carried mail and cargo. Between 1910 and 1914, DELAG carried 34,228 passengers on 1,588 flights. There were some accidents, and seven ships were destroyed. But not a single person was killed or even badly hurt.

Zeppelins might have become a common way to travel all over Europe. But history got in the way. In 1914, World War I broke out, with Germany at the center.

CHAPTER 5
Zeppelins in the War

With war coming, the army finally became interested in zeppelins. By 1913, the German army and navy were beginning to build up a fleet of airships. Zeppelin's little factory became a big business.

World War I

In 1871, a group of small kingdoms joined to form the German Empire. The new empire wanted to show the world how strong it was. This caused conflicts all over Eastern Europe.

In 1914, Archduke Franz Ferdinand of Austria-Hungary was killed by a Serbian. Austria-Hungary invaded Serbia. Germany was an ally of Austria-Hungary, so it joined the fight. Russia was an ally of Serbia, so it joined on the other side. Other allies joined in on both sides. Soon most of the world was at war. On one side were Germany and Austria-Hungary and their allies. They lost the war in 1918 to England, France, Russia, and their allies. (The United States did not enter the war against Germany until 1917.)

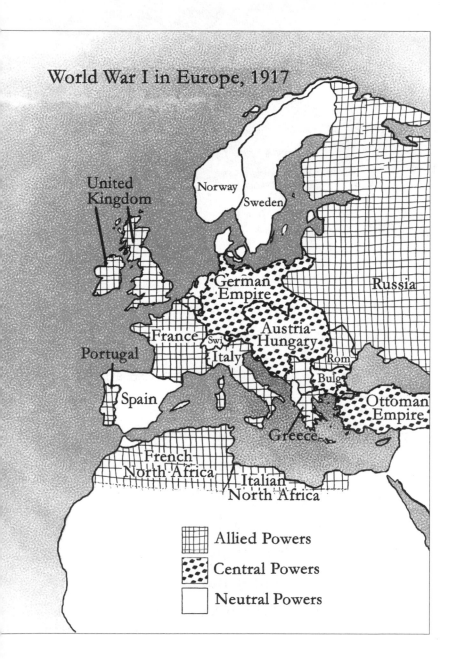

World War I in Europe, 1917

Allied Powers

Central Powers

Neutral Powers

The military was beginning to use airplanes, as well. But zeppelins could go higher than any airplane. They could fly high enough to stay out of the reach of fighter planes. They could carry a lot more weight than an airplane. Also, most airplanes could fly for only two or three hours without having to land. This meant they could go only a few hundred miles. But a zeppelin could fly for days. One flew 4,225 miles nonstop. Zeppelins could carry soldiers, supplies, or weapons far into enemy territory.

Airships were used in several ways during the war. Riding in one, a scout could find out what the landscape was like, and what the enemy army was doing. He could report the location of enemy ships. Airships were especially good at carrying supplies over long distances.

In the spring of 1915, the Germans began sending zeppelins to bomb London. The English were helpless to stop them. The zeppelins flew too high for their planes to attack. If a fighter plane did manage to shoot a zeppelin, it didn't make much difference. The bullet would just make a hole in one of the balloon's many gas cells. The hydrogen in that cell would leak out, and the zeppelin would sink a bit. But it could still fly home. Until now, London had been too far from Germany for bombers to reach it easily. Now no place was safe.

Zeppelins were so important to the German army that they changed the German diet. The cells holding the hydrogen were lined with cow intestines. It took the intestines of 250,000 cows to line one ship. In peacetime, cow intestines were mainly used for sausage casings. The government wanted to be sure there were enough intestines to make zeppelins—so it became illegal to make sausages in Germany or any country Germany controlled.

Fortunately, after a few years, the English
figured out how to deal with zeppelins. They
developed a new kind of bullet that broke into
flames when it was shot. When these bullets hit
a zeppelin, they set fire to the hydrogen inside.
Then the whole ship would burn. Zeppelins
didn't help the Germans in World War I nearly as
much as they had hoped.

CHAPTER 6
No More Zeppelins for Germany

Count Zeppelin died in 1917 at the age of seventy-eight, soon before Germany lost World War I. After a few years, Eckener became the head of the Zeppelin Company. The company hoped to start up its commercial airline again. It built two new, improved zeppelins and began regular flights.

But the treaty signed after the war said Germany had to give all of its airships to the victorious Allied nations. Even the two new zeppelins had to be given away. Germany was not allowed to build any more large airships. With nothing else to do, the Zeppelin Company started to make cooking pots from its aluminum.

Eckener saved the company with a brilliant idea. When Germany's zeppelins had been divided

among the victorious countries, none of them went to the United States. The United States was having trouble building its own airships. No one knew more about building zeppelins than the Zeppelin Company. So in 1924, Eckener asked if Germany could build zeppelins for the United States.

The American government jumped at the chance. Now the Zeppelin Company could do what Eckener wanted most—make bigger and better airships. It wouldn't get to keep the ships. But at least it would have a chance to experiment with new ideas.

In October 1924, the first new zeppelin was finished. Named the *Los Angeles,* it flew across the Atlantic Ocean to New Jersey in about four days.

An engraving of the first hot-air balloon flight

Studio photograph of a passenger in a hot-air balloon

Ferdinand, Graf von Zeppelin

An early airship in flight

Hugo Eckener

Lounge area of the *Hindenburg*

Dining area of the *Hindenburg*

The Reading and Writing Room on the *Hindenburg*

The *Hindenburg* flying over the Olympic Stadium
outside Berlin, Germany, during the 1936 Games

Soldiers helping to land the *Hindenburg* in Frankfurt, Germany,
after a record-breaking forty-eight-hour flight

The *Hindenburg* entering the US Navy hangar in Lakehurst, New Jersey, on May 9, 1936, after its first North Atlantic crossing

The *Hindenburg* floating near the
Empire State Building on August 8, 1936

The *Hindenburg* flying over lower Manhattan on its first transatlantic flight

Flames engulfing the *Hindenburg* on May 6, 1937

Rescuers rushing to save passengers and crew of the *Hindenburg*

A survivor of the crash being led away

The aftermath of the *Hindenburg* crash

The front page of the *New York Times* the day after the crash

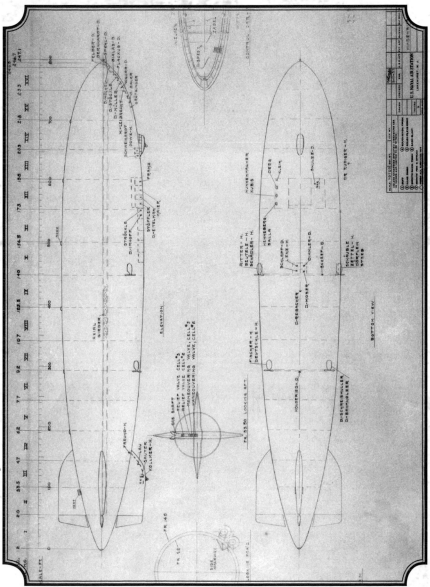

A drawing of the *Hindenburg* showing the stations of officers and crew at the time of the disaster, used in the investigation of the crash

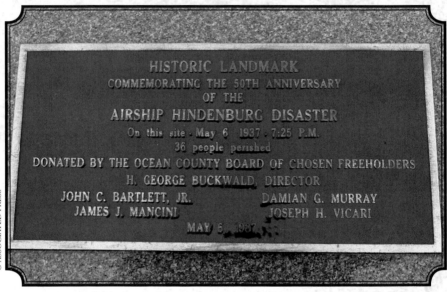

A fiftieth-anniversary memorial plaque marking the
spot in Lakehurst, New Jersey, where the *Hindenburg* burned

This ship had one important difference that made it safer than any other zeppelin: It was not designed to be filled with hydrogen. Instead, the new zeppelin could be filled with helium. Hydrogen bursts into flames easily. Zeppelin builders had to be very careful to protect the hydrogen cells so that not even a single spark reached them. But helium doesn't burn.

The worst danger to a zeppelin was fire. Even if a ship was badly hurt in midair, the people on board would probably survive. When a lighter-than-air ship was damaged, it didn't fall to the ground at a dangerous speed, the way an airplane would. The gas that held it up was stored in many different cells. Unless every single cell was destroyed, there would still be enough gas to help hold up the ship. It would float down slowly, like a partly empty helium balloon. But if even one spark reached the hydrogen that filled the balloon, the ship would burst into flames. That was what killed people.

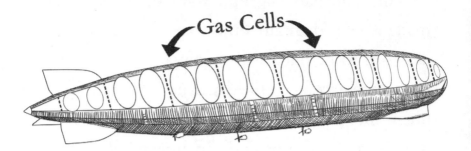

Gas Cells

Clearly helium airships would be much safer than hydrogen ships. So why didn't all airships use helium? Unfortunately, helium is very expensive and very rare. Most of the world's helium is in the United States. Germany would have liked to use helium, but it couldn't get any.

The *Los Angeles* was used by the US Navy until 1932, and then retired, still in good shape.

CHAPTER 7
The Golden Age

The years after the war were the golden age of airships. Many countries began to build their own. An airship built in England was the first to cross the Atlantic Ocean, in July 1919. On May 12, 1926, an airship built by Norway and Italy became the first vessel of any kind to fly over the North Pole. (An American airplane pilot claimed he had beaten them by three days, but he probably did not actually reach the pole.)

The first rigid airship built in America was the *Shenandoah*. In 1924, it became the first lighter-than-air vessel to cross North America. The government wanted Americans all over the country to admire it. Its second trip across the continent was less fortunate. In September 1925, the *Shenandoah* ran in a powerful thunderstorm, which broke the ship into three pieces. Since it was filled with helium, it did not burst into flames. But the control car that hung from the balloon broke away. Without any gas to hold it up, it fell rapidly to earth. Everyone in it was killed. The back end of the balloon held the engines. The weight of the engines dragged it down. But there was still gas in the balloon, so it fell very slowly. All of the men in it survived. However, the front end, with no engines, was so light that it shot 10,000 feet up into the air. The men riding in it were then able to take control and pilot it back to earth, flying it like a balloon. They also survived.

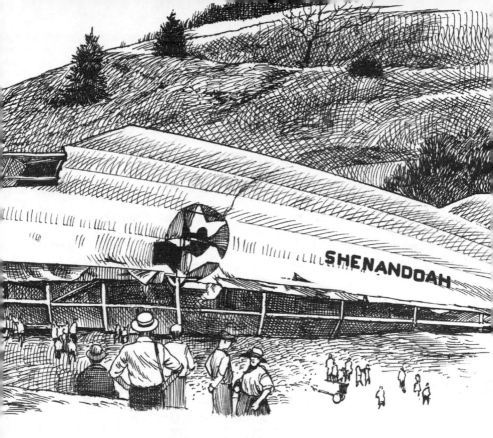

In the meantime, back in Germany, the Zeppelin Company was now allowed to begin building its own zeppelins again. It formed a partnership with an American firm, the Goodyear Tire & Rubber Company. In 1926, Goodyear-Zeppelin began work on the most successful airship of all time.

The new ship was named the *Graf Zeppelin*, in honor of the company's founder. (*Graf* is the German word for count.) In nine years, the *Graf Zeppelin* flew more than one million miles and carried more than 34,000 passengers. In all that time, not a single passenger or crew member was ever hurt or killed.

The company planned for the *Graf Zeppelin* to be the first airship to carry customers across the ocean. They hoped to become the main carrier between Europe and America. In the 1920s, only ocean liners made the journey across the Atlantic. People thought that airplanes would never be big or strong enough to carry passengers such a long distance. It was barely possible for an airplane to cross the ocean nonstop. But it was dangerous and difficult. And in order to carry enough fuel, the plane couldn't carry anything else except the pilot. So for commercial flights across the Atlantic Ocean, everyone was sure that airships were the right choice.

Airplane Flights Across the Atlantic

The very first flight across the Atlantic was made by an airplane, two months before an airship made the crossing. In May 1919, the US Navy sent three

airplanes from Newfoundland to England. Only one plane made it. It had to stop six times on the way to refuel. The first nonstop flight across the Atlantic was made by two British pilots a month later. They also took off from Newfoundland, because it is the farthest point east in North America. This made the journey shorter. Sixteen hours later, they crashed in a bog in Ireland.

On May 20, 1927, American pilot Charles Lindbergh left New York in an airplane named the *Spirit of St. Louis*. He completed the first nonstop solo flight across the Atlantic, going from New York to Paris in thirty-three and a half hours.

The Zeppelin Company wanted people to trust their new ship. So they sent it on special display trips to show it off. The *Graf Zeppelin*'s most dramatic publicity stunt was a flight all the way around the world in 1929. Because the trip was partly paid for by an American newspaper, it began and ended in Lakehurst, New Jersey. Lakehurst was chosen because it was the nearest place to New York where there was room to land such a large ship.

The trip took twelve days of actual flying time. One leg was a flight from Tokyo to California. Eckener made sure the arrival would be as dramatic as possible. He carefully timed the trip

so the ship would fly in through San Francisco's Golden Gate just at sunset.

The *Graf Zeppelin* made several other special flights. These included a research flight over the North Pole. Then, in the summer of 1931, it began to carry paying passengers from Germany to Brazil. The company wanted to be sure everything was working perfectly before a zeppelin crossed the Atlantic to land in New York, where all the world would be watching.

After a successful season of flights to South America, it was time to begin offering trips between Germany and the United States. So the company began building the biggest, most elegant zeppelin ever—the *Hindenburg*.

CHAPTER 8
The *Hindenburg*

The *Hindenburg* was named after Paul Hindenburg. He was a much-loved World War I hero and the former president of Germany. The *Hindenburg* is still the largest object that has ever flown. Built between 1931 and 1936, it was 804 feet long—almost the length of three football fields. It was 135 feet high, about the height of a twelve-story building. It could fly more than eighty miles per hour, carrying one hundred people.

Paul Hindenburg

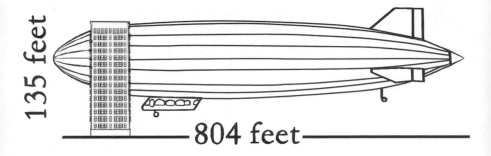

135 feet

804 feet

By the 1930s, when the *Hindenburg* was being built, the Nazis were beginning to seize power in Germany. Eckener was no friend of the Nazis. He gave speeches supporting their opponents and publicly made fun of the Nazi salute. He would not let Hitler hold a political rally in a zeppelin shed. In 1933, Eckener flew the *Graf Zeppelin* over the Chicago World's Fair. The airship was required to display a swastika, the symbol of the Nazi government, on its left fin. But Eckener made sure to fly in a clockwise circle, so no one at the fair could see it.

Almost no one in Germany could safely speak out against the Nazis. However, Eckener was one of the most beloved heroes in Germany. People even suggested that he should run for president of Germany. They thought he might be strong enough to stand up to Hitler. But Eckener wasn't interested in politics.

Hitler didn't like zeppelins. But he understood how useful they could be. His government gave the company the money it needed to build the *Hindenburg*. But he wanted to be sure the person in charge of the Zeppelin Company supported him. The Nazis moved in and weakened Eckener's control.

The Zeppelin Company wanted the *Hindenburg* to use helium, because it was so much safer. As the Nazis rose to power, however, the United States trusted Germany less and less. The American government refused to sell any helium to Nazi Germany. So the *Hindenburg* had to use hydrogen.

In March 1936, the *Hindenburg* was finished. Hitler decided to use it and the *Graf Zeppelin* for his own purposes.

He wanted the German people to see the two largest airships in the world supporting him. They would remind people how strong Nazi Germany

Adolf Hitler

was. Hitler ordered the zeppelins to fly around the country playing patriotic music and broadcasting propaganda. Eckener refused. However, Eckener no longer had the power to stop the Nazis. The *Hindenburg* spent the next four days campaigning for Hitler instead of completing security tests.

Two days later, the *Hindenburg* set off on its first transatlantic passenger flight. It flew to Brazil rather than the United States, as a trial run before the important trip to New York. Because of Hitler's propaganda flights, there had never been time to test the engines. One engine broke down on the trip out, and two failed on the trip back. For the first time, Eckener was not the pilot on the opening voyage of one of his ships. He had been eased out. He went along only as a private citizen.

CHAPTER 9
A Magical Flight

On May 6, 1936, the *Hindenburg* left for its first passenger flight between Europe and the United States. Eckener was aboard as a private passenger. The one-way trip cost $400, which was a lot of money. But the passengers thought it was worth it. They knew they were making history.

Nothing today comes close to the experience of flying on the *Hindenburg*. It was not at all like flying on an airplane. It had twenty-five tiny cabins.

Two people slept in each one, in bunk beds. A little table and a sink with hot and cold running water could be folded into the wall to make more room. There was also a room where people could shower.

Passengers could gather in several elegant public rooms. A promenade ran all along both sides of the ship. It had comfortable chairs and huge, slanting windows that could be opened. The passengers sat there to watch the scenery pass by. The lounge had a bar and a grand piano. A map of the world was painted on the wall. It showed the routes of famous explorers. Next door was a quiet room for people who wanted to read or write.

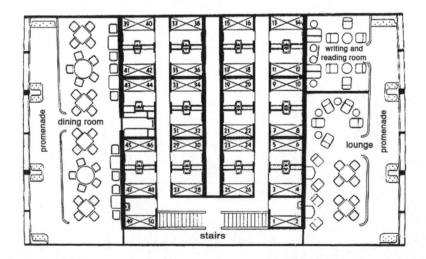

The dining room had fresh flowers, tablecloths, and elegant china and silver. The food was fancy. The menu included dishes like fattened duckling, Bavarian-style. The kitchen staff packed 440 pounds of fresh meat, 220 pounds of butter, and 800 eggs for the flight.

There was even a smoking room. Any stray spark on a zeppelin could ignite the ship's hydrogen. Smoking on one seems like a terrible idea. But smoking was part of elegant living in the 1930s. The smoking room was protected by an air lock that kept it separate from the rest of the ship. An attendant let people in and out. Inside, there was one electric lighter that everyone had to use. The smoking room was one of the most popular places on the ship.

Of course everything on board had to weigh as little as possible. The chairs were made of hollow aluminum tubes. The walls of the bedrooms were nothing but foam covered by a layer of fabric. Even the piano was made of aluminum, covered with pigskin.

Passengers found the flight a magical experience. The ship rose into the air so lightly that people on board couldn't even tell when it took off. It was almost silent. The motion was completely smooth. One man said it was like being carried in an angel's arms. Another compared it to hanging from a star while the earth turned beneath him.

A crew member called the elevator man kept the ship on an even path up and down by changing the angle of the ship's nose. During a storm and at takeoff and landing, this took great skill. For most of the flight, his job was simply to keep the passengers comfortable. He watched a bubble suspended in fluid on the control panel, and tried to keep it centered. He wanted the ship to stay so level that a glass of wine would not spill.

The first flight was smooth and uneventful. As the ship flew over New York, it was greeted with horns and steamship whistles. The pilot flew so low past the Empire State Building that the passengers could wave to people standing on the observation deck. It landed easily, and took off on its return flight the same day.

The Empire State Building

When the Empire State Building was built in 1931, it had a mooring mast on top for airships. The idea was that, instead of having to land in New Jersey, passengers would walk down a gangplank to the top of the skyscraper in the middle of Manhattan. This was not a realistic plan. It would be very dangerous to get out of an airship hanging 1,454 feet above the ground. So the mooring mast was never used. But its extra height made the Empire State Building the world's tallest building for forty years.

Mooring Mast

The *Hindenburg* made the trip between Germany and America twenty times that year. It ended the season with the "Millionaires' Flight." Seventy-two of the richest and most powerful men in America were invited on board for a sightseeing trip. One of the guests was Eddie Rickenbacker. He was a famous World War I pilot who had fought against the Germans. Now he was flying on a German airship.

Eddie
Rickenbacker

CHAPTER 10
The Final Voyage

The *Hindenburg*'s first season was a complete success. Almost every flight had been full. There had been no problems. The Zeppelin Company began planning for a future in which airships would carry people all over the world. They hoped to have as many as forty zeppelins in the sky by 1945.

On May 3, 1937, the first flight of the *Hindenburg*'s second season took off from Germany. The trip to New York was only a little more than half full. This time, Eckener stayed home altogether. There were some Nazi officers onboard. But the passengers were mostly businessmen, students, retired couples, and journalists.

The crew made clear that safety was important.

Luggage was weighed to make sure it wouldn't overload the ship. Cigarette lighters, matches, and flashbulbs were taken away from the passengers. Nothing that might make sparks was allowed on board. Eight-year-old Werner Doehner and his ten-year-old brother, Walter, 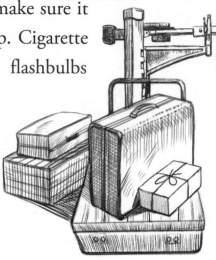 had a toy tank. Its wheels made sparks when they played with it. When the steward saw it, he took it away. He carefully explained to the little boys how dangerous sparks could be.

The trip was not very exciting. It was cloudy most of the way, so there was no view. A couple of thunderstorms slowed things down. On May 6, after three days, the *Hindenburg* reached North America. It was running hours late. And it was supposed to turn around and go back to Europe that same night. The flight back was completely booked with people who were going to England for the crowning of King George VI.

The captain grew impatient. However, the ground crew told him the weather in New Jersey was too bad to land. He took his passengers on a tour flying low over Manhattan to kill time. Finally, he was told that it was safe, and the airship rushed to the field.

The captain was in a hurry. As he approached the landing field, he turned the ship a little too sharply. But it didn't seem to do any harm. Then he noticed that the back end of the ship was a bit low. He dropped some water to make it lighter. It was still too heavy. That was odd. To fix it, he dropped water a second time. To the amusement of the passengers watching from the windows, some of the water hit the crowd of observers who were waiting below. The back stayed low, although it didn't seem to be causing any problems. The whole crew had a lot of experience with zeppelins. They knew that little things went wrong all the time. It was nothing to worry about.

The ship floated gently down toward the mooring post. When it was low enough, crew members dropped heavy ropes down to the men on the ground. They would haul in the airship. The *Hindenburg* hung in perfect stillness. To the people below, it looked like a cloud or a jewel in the sky. Passengers leaned out the windows, calling to their friends on the ground. It seemed the *Hindenburg* had arrived successfully again. Its safety record was still unbroken.

Then, at 7:25 p.m., there was a strange *whoosh*.

CHAPTER 11
A Torch in Midair

The four crew members in the back fin looked up just as the gas cell nearest them exploded into flames, and the fire began racing toward them. Suddenly, people on the ground saw a tiny, mushroom-shaped flame burst from the back of the airship. In the control car, the captain felt a jolt. He couldn't imagine what it was. Then one of his officers looked out the window and cried out. The back of the ship was on fire! There was nothing anyone could do. The flames raced from one hydrogen cell to the next, toward the front of the ship. Within a few seconds, the *Hindenburg* was blazing like a torch in midair.

As the hydrogen that held it up burned away, the back of the ship plunged toward the earth. Then the front went down. Watchers on the ground saw burning bodies falling from the ship. The whole disaster was so sudden. One second, everything had seemed perfectly calm and normal. The next, all 804 feet of the *Hindenburg* were wrapped in flames. From the first spark to the final crash, the entire disaster lasted only thirty-four seconds.

Herbert Morrison, a Chicago reporter, was at the airfield, describing the *Hindenburg*'s landing for a later radio broadcast. His emotional reaction to the tragedy was captured on a recording as it happened. It was played all over the country. He was calmly describing the landing, when suddenly he cried out: "It burst into flames! . . . It's fire—and it's crashing! It's crashing terrible! . . . It's burning and bursting into flames, and the . . . this is terrible, this is one of the worst catastrophes in the world . . . It's smoke, and it's flames now . . . and the frame is crashing to the ground . . . Oh, the humanity and all the passengers screaming . . ." The entire accident was also caught on film.

The people on board had only a few seconds to

react. Breaking open windows or tearing through the fabric of the balloon, they leaped from the burning ship as it fell. Some jumped while the ship was still too high. They died when they hit the ground. Others waited too long and were killed in the fire. Some managed to jump safely, but were then killed when wreckage fell on top of them. The luckiest survived.

The death toll of the *Hindenburg* was not as terrible as it might have been. Thirty-five passengers and crew members died, as well as one unlucky member of the ground crew. Remarkably, of the ninety-seven people who had been onboard the *Hindenburg*, sixty-two of them—almost two-thirds—survived. Among them was Captain Max Pruss, who stayed on board till the ship hit the ground and helped rescue passengers.

Captain Max Pruss

Letters from the *Hindenburg*

Many of the Zeppelin Company's flights earned money by delivering souvenir mail. Collectors were willing to pay a lot of money for letters postmarked on board a famous airship. The *Hindenburg* was carrying a large number of these letters when it crashed. Amazingly, many of them survived the fire. As many as possible were delivered; scorched, but still legible. These letters are now worth a lot of money.

t Luftschiff "Hindenburg"

enker & CO. G.m.b.H.
Zweigniederlassung
Frankfurt a. M. 17
Hafenstraße 53   55

Messrs,
A.F.Cofod & Co.,
24, State Street,
NEW YORK NY

Every survivor had a unique story. The two
young children on board, Werner and Walter
Doehner, were thrown out the window by their
mother. A steward waiting below caught them in
his arms. Both lived, as did their mother. However,
their father and fourteen-year-old sister died.

Fourteen-year-old Werner Franz was a cabin
boy. When the fire broke out, he was putting
away dishes. As he raced from the flames, a tank
burst above him, soaking him with water. He

was so wet that he was able to race through the fire and escape without injury. The next day, he went back to the wrecked ship. He found the remains of the bunk where he had slept, and rescued a watch that had been given to him by his grandfather.

Sixty-one-year-old Marie Kleemann was hurrying to America to take care of her sick daughter. When the ship burst into flames, she was completely bewildered. She simply sat in the dining room, watching the chaos around her. One of the ship's stewards, Fritz Deeg, who had jumped to safety, went back into the burning ship to see if he could help anyone. He found Marie and led her down the gangplank stairs. She was unharmed and still clutching her gloves. Deeg then returned and helped other passengers down.

CHAPTER 12
What Went Wrong?

The *Hindenburg* was certainly not the first airship to go up in flames. Nor was it the most deadly airship accident. The American airship *Akron* had been destroyed in a thunderstorm in 1933. Seventy-three of the seventy-six people on board were killed.

However, the destruction of the *Hindenburg* frightened people more than any other airship disaster. One reason for this was the firsthand way the public experienced it. Before, people had learned about accidents after they happened. They heard the destruction of the *Hindenburg* described second by second as it took place, by a radio reporter who wept in horror. And the whole thing was filmed, so people could watch every detail. This made it seem frighteningly real.

The *Hindenburg* was also the first civilian airship disaster. Earlier accidents had happened during experimental or military flights. In the twenty-eight years since Count Zeppelin had started his little airline, not a single passenger on a

commercial airship flight had ever been killed.

One other thing made the *Hindenburg*'s destruction so upsetting: No one knew what caused it. Many crew members, including the captain, believed someone must have planned the accident. Everything had been going so smoothly. They knew how safe the ship was. They didn't think a fire could have started by chance. Maybe someone who hated the Nazis had decided to destroy the ship because it was a symbol of the

Nazis' power. But no one has ever been able to prove this.

After a careful investigation, a US government commission decided that somehow, a hydrogen leak had started. Maybe the sharp turn before landing had broken a wire that tore a hole in a gas cell. Then a spark had started the fire. The spark might have come from electricity in the air after the thunderstorm. It might have had something to do with the substance used to coat the fabric on the outside of the ship. It might have traveled up from the earth when the crew threw down the mooring ropes. Or there might have been some other reason. We will probably never know exactly what made the *Hindenburg* burst into flames.

The *Hindenburg* was supposed to show the world how powerful the Nazis were. Its destruction was a big blow to Germany.

CHAPTER 13
The Death of the Zeppelin

The destruction of the *Hindenburg* was a death sentence for lighter-than-air ships. No one wanted to fly in a ship filled with hydrogen ever again. The world had watched and listened as the huge ship went up in flames. That made the image too vivid to forget.

The *Hindenburg*, however, was not the very last zeppelin. The Nazis were not ready to give up. They built one final ship, which they again named the *Graf Zeppelin*. It never did much. Hitler used it, as he had the *Hindenburg*, to drop leaflets urging people to support him. And the German government tried to use it to spy on England.

In 1940, the Nazis had the new *Graf*

Zeppelin destroyed, along with the original *Graf Zeppelin*. Their metal framework was recycled to build airplanes.

Airplanes were ready to take over from

airships. In 1930, the powerful jet engine had been invented, and soon it was replacing the propeller engine. Airplanes could now fly long distances and carry heavy weights. They were much faster than airships. Even the fastest of the Zeppelin Company's ships had never reached a speed of 100 miles per hour. The fastest World War I airplane could fly 146 miles per hour. Most passenger planes today travel at 500 to 600 miles per hour.

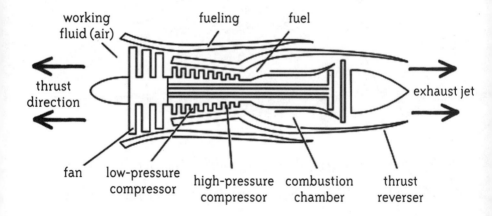

The first land-based transatlantic airplane
passenger flight took place in 1938. It flew from
Berlin to New York. This was only a year and a
half after the *Hindenburg* was destroyed. Even
Hugo Eckener admitted that airplanes now made
more sense than lighter-than-air ships.

Modern Zeppelins

The dream of a sky filled with zeppelins never completely died. Since 1989, a branch of the Zeppelin Company has been working on a new kind of airship. It is called the Zeppelin NT, for "new technology."

This ship uses helium, which is much safer than hydrogen. Because helium is expensive and very hard to get, these new zeppelins will be smaller than the old ones. Engineers think they will be useful for flying to hard-to-reach areas and carrying heavy equipment. Starting in early 2014, Goodyear plans to start using Zeppelin NTs instead of blimps.

Yet the airships floating serenely, so completely at home in the air, had a special beauty that nothing can replace. Looking back after the last zeppelin had been grounded, Eckener remembered the "lightness and grace" of his beloved ships. He described how they "seemed to be coming from another world and to be returning there like a dream . . ." Not so long ago, people dreamed that zeppelins would one day fill the sky. They imagined that traveling would mean floating through the air as easily as if we belonged there. With the fiery destruction of the *Hindenburg*, that dream vanished.

Timeline of the *Hindenburg*

1783	First manned hot-air balloon flight takes place, followed by first hydrogen balloon flight
1852	First steerable balloon ship is flown for seventeen miles
1885	Gottlieb Daimler patents a light, gasoline-burning engine
1897	First aluminum airship crashes on first flight
1900	Ferdinand Graf von Zeppelin builds his first airship, LZ-1
1909	Zeppelin founds DELAG, the world's first airline
1915	German zeppelins bomb London
1919	An English airship becomes the first to cross the Atlantic Ocean
1924	Zeppelin company agrees to build airships for the United States
1926	Airship crosses the North Pole during a scientific expedition
1929	*Graf Zeppelin* flies all the way around the world
1931	Construction of the *Hindenburg* begins
1933	*Graf Zeppelin* seen by thousands as it flies over the Chicago World's Fair
1937	*Hindenburg* explodes upon landing in America
1940	Nazis destroy Germany's last zeppelins for scrap metal
1989	Zeppelin company begins work on Zeppelin NT ("new technology")
2014	Goodyear intends to replace its blimps with Zeppelin NTs by the end of this year

Timeline of the World

End of the American Revolution	1783
Japan is opened to trade with Western countries for the first time in modern history	1854
American Civil War begins	1861
Adolf Hitler is born	1889
Construction of New York subway begins	1900
Wright brothers make the first airplane flight, at Kitty Hawk	1903
World War I begins	1914
Two British pilots make the first flight across the Atlantic by airplane	1919
American pilot Charles Lindbergh makes the world's first nonstop solo flight across the Atlantic	1927
Crash of the American stock market begins the Great Depression	1929
Invention of the jet engine	1930
Empire State Building completed	1931
Nazi Party seizes power in Germany	1933
Amelia Earhart vanishes while trying to become the first woman to fly a plane around the world	1937
First regular transatlantic airplane passenger service begins	1939
World War II begins	
World War II ends	1945
Apollo 11 astronaut Neil Armstrong becomes first person to walk on the moon	1969
NASA flies the final Space Shuttle mission	2011

Bibliography

*Books for young readers

Archbold, Rick. Hindenburg: *An Illustrated History*. New York: Warner Books, 1994.

Bingham, Jane. *The* Hindenburg *1937: A Huge Airship Is Destroyed by Fire*. Chicago: Raintree, 2006.

Dick, Harold G., with Douglas H. Robertson. *The Golden Age of the Great Passenger Airships:* Graf Zeppelin *and* Hindenburg. Washington, DC: Smithsonian Books, 1992.

Lace, William W. *The* Hindenburg *Disaster of 1937*. New York: Chelsea House, 2008.

*Majoor, Mireille. Illustrations by Ken Marschall. *Inside the* Hindenburg: *Giant Cutaway Book*. New York: Madison Press, 2000.

Websites

Airships: The *Hindenburg* and Other Zeppelins.
    http://www.airships.net/

Faces of the *Hindenburg*: Biographic Information on Each of the 97 Persons Who Were Aboard the Passenger Airship *Hindenburg*.
    http://facesofthehindenburg.blogspot.com